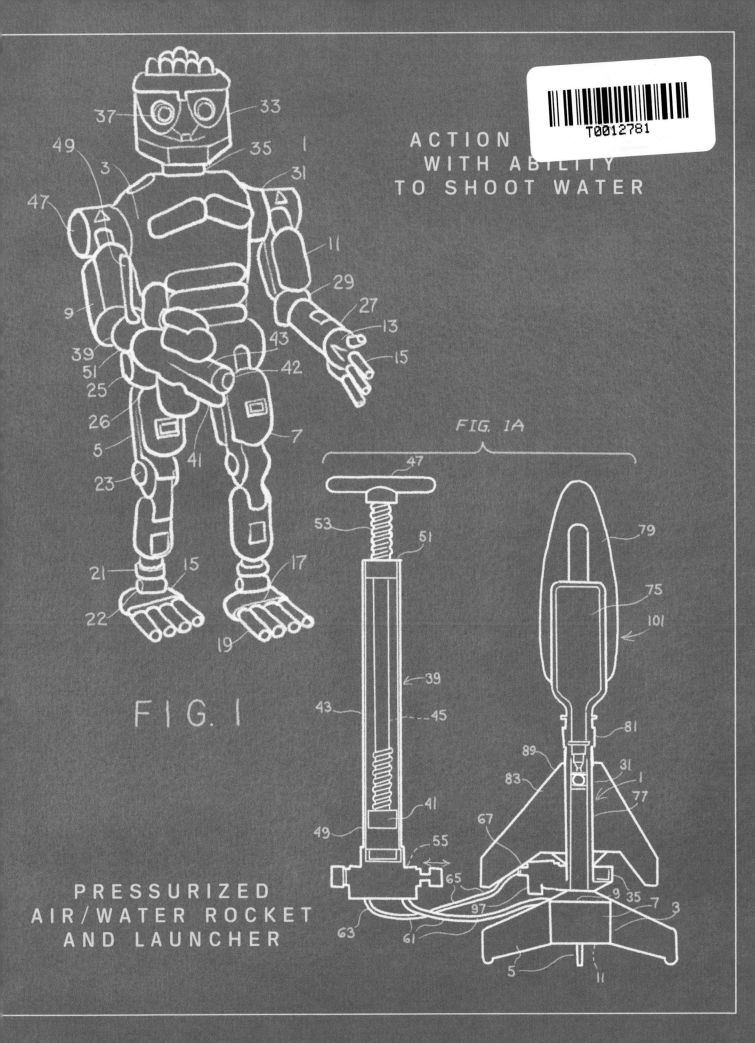

ACTION
WITH ABILITY
TO SHOOT WATER

FIG. 1A

FIG. 1

PRESSURIZED
AIR/WATER ROCKET
AND LAUNCHER

WHOOSH!

Lonnie Johnson's
SUPER–SOAKING
Stream of Inventions

Chris Barton • Illustrated by **Don Tate**

ini Charlesbridge

For Fletcher
—C. B.

For every kid with big ideas
—D. T.

First paperback edition 2019
Text copyright © 2016 by Chris Barton
Illustrations copyright © 2016 by Don Tate
All rights reserved, including the right of reproduction in whole or in part in any form.
Charlesbridge and colophon are registered trademarks of Charlesbridge Publishing, Inc.

Published by Charlesbridge
9 Galen Street
Watertown, MA 02472
(617) 926-0329
www.charlesbridge.com

Library of Congress Cataloging-in-Publication Data
Barton, Chris, author.
   Whoosh!: Lonnie Johnson's super-soaking stream of inventions / Chris Barton;
illustrated by Don Tate.
      pages cm
   ISBN 978-1-58089-297-1 (reinforced for library use)
   ISBN 978-1-58089-298-8 (softcover)
   ISBN 978-1-60734-640-1 (ebook)
   ISBN 978-1-60734-854-2 (ebook pdf)
1. Johnson, Lonnie, 1949– —Juvenile literature. 2. African American
inventors—Alabama—Biography—Juvenile literature. 3. Inventors—
United States—Biography—Juvenile literature. 4. African Americans—
Alabama—Biography—Juvenile literature. I. Tate, Don, illustrator.
II. Title.

T40.J585B37 2016
609.2—dc23
[B]   2015017342

Printed in China
(hc) 15 14 13 12
(sc) 10 9 8 7 6 5

Illustrations created digitally using Manga Studio
Display type set in Space Toaster by Chank
Text type set in ITC Goudy Sans by Bitstream Inc.
Color separations by Colourscan Print Co Pte Ltd, Singapore
Printed by 1010 Printing International Limited in Huizhou, Guangdong, China
Production supervision by Brian G. Walker
Designed by Diane M. Earley

EVERY DAY brought a challenge for young Lonnie
Johnson—the challenge of finding space for his stuff.
Six Johnson kids were squeezed into their parents' small
house in Mobile, Alabama. Lonnie would have loved
a workshop of his own, but there just wasn't room.
There was nowhere to keep his rocket kits . . .

bamboo shooters . . .

rubber-band guns . . .

Erector set . . .

go-kart engine . . .

bolts and screws and other spare parts his dad let
him bring in from the shed, and various other things
he'd hauled back from the junkyard.

Lonnie loved building and creating. Ideas for inventions just kept on flowing.

He learned how to make rockets from scratch.
Kids at school gathered to watch Lonnie launch them.
And he learned how to make rocket fuel. When it
caught fire in the kitchen, Lonnie's mom didn't make
him stop. She just sent him to work outside.

Lonnie wanted to spend his life designing things, building things, and getting them to work. He wanted to be an engineer. However, Lonnie took an exam that said he would not make a very good one.

His dream had been challenged. Lonnie was discouraged. But he knew that whoever had graded his test hadn't met Linex.

Inspired by a TV show, Lonnie had built his own robot. He made it out of scrap metal and named it Linex.

Compressed-air cylinders and valves allowed Linex's body to turn and its arms to move. The switches came from an old, broken jukebox. Lonnie used a tape recorder to program Linex, and as a bonus the reels looked like eyes. Lonnie wanted to enter his creation in a science fair, but he couldn't get the transmitter to work. Without it Lonnie couldn't send commands to Linex.

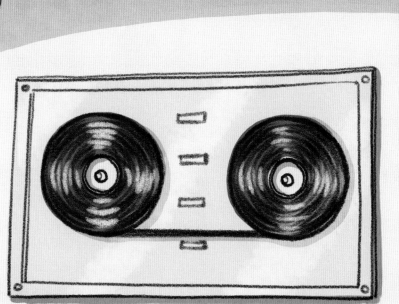

Science fairs came and went. Lonnie missed one
and then another—until he got an idea.
Now, Lonnie may or may not have asked before he
borrowed his little sister's walkie-talkie . . .

. . . but it fixed the transmission issue. His school's team took freshly finished Linex to a 1968 science fair at the University of Alabama—where only five years earlier, African American students hadn't even been allowed.

Having to compete in a place that still wasn't very welcoming? Now, *that* was a challenge with a capital C. Against other schools from all over the state, Lonnie's team won first place.

Soon Lonnie left home to go to college at Tuskegee Institute, where he stood out as a self-confident, insightful, creative thinker.

He stood out as a student who asked the right questions, precisely defined problems, and formulated solutions.

And he stood out as the guy who built his own booming sound system out of cast-off electronics. It even had lights that flashed in sync with the beat.

Lonnie sometimes studied right in the middle of his own parties. The extra studying paid off. He became an engineer after graduation, and that took him beyond Alabama—*way* beyond.

When NASA was sending an orbiter and probe called *Galileo* to Jupiter, the space agency needed to ensure a constant supply of power to the orbiter's computer memory. The engineer who had to figure out how to do it was Lonnie.

GALILEO

LOW-GAIN ANTENNA

SUN SHIELDS

THRUSTERS

PROBE RELAY ANTENNA

SCAN PLATFORM

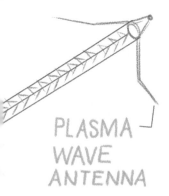

PLASMA
WAVE
ANTENNA

TROPROPULSION
MODULE

JUPITER
PROBE

His challenge was to come up with a lightweight
backup system able to keep essential functions going
in case the main power was lost.

It wasn't easy. It wasn't obvious. But Lonnie found
a solution.

Some at NASA's Jet Propulsion Laboratory doubted
his idea would work. Lonnie convinced them it would.

He was right.

As it photographed Jupiter and its moons, *Galileo* was
supported by the power package that Lonnie designed.
Much of what we know about Jupiter could have been
at risk in a power failure if not for Lonnie.

Ideas for other problems to solve just kept on flowing. They flowed whether Lonnie was working with hundreds of people at NASA or up late tinkering with his own inventions in—finally!—his own workshop.

Lonnie knew the world's millions of refrigerators and air conditioners needed a new cooling system—one that didn't use R-12, a chemical that was bad for the environment. He had an idea for using water and air pressure instead.

To test his idea, he made a pump and nozzle . . . connected them to the bathroom faucet . . . turned on the faucet, turned on the pump, and then . . .

The stream that blasted across the bathroom was so powerful, it created a curtain-swirling breeze. It also gave Lonnie an idea for yet another invention.

"This," he thought, "would make a great water gun."

First he had to find or make the parts, including a pump small enough for a child to handle.

Then he had to glue the parts together into a prototype— an early version with room for improvement.

Finally Lonnie tested his strange-looking squirt gun at a picnic.

"Does it really work?" a man asked.

"Sure," Lonnie said. "Wanna see?"

Lonnie worked the pump, which squeezed air into a chamber. When he pulled the trigger, the air escaped, forcing water out with a . . .

W H O

For a water battle to be a fair fight, there couldn't be just one of Lonnie's water guns. He needed help making more.

So, he went to toy company . . .

after toy company . . .

after toy company.

YES! ⚡

The word "no" flowed again and again. But finally one company said, "Yes!" It planned to make his water gun! Lonnie also had other projects: a water-propelled toy airplane, two kinds of engines, and his cooling system. He found investors to provide the money for turning his ideas into products people could buy. He made a leap of faith, quit his day job, and devoted himself to full-time inventing.

But soon each plan fell apart—even the one for the water gun. These things sometimes happen. But when they happen one after another to the same person—well, that's some pretty bad luck.

Lonnie didn't have a job. He didn't have the money he'd been counting on. He and his family had to move out of their home and into a little apartment. He was angry and scared.

But Lonnie had dealt with challenges all his life. He knew a lot about solving problems. And he still believed in his inventions, especially the water gun. Lonnie went looking for another toy company.

WATER GUN PARTS

In 1989 he found a toy maker who was interested in seeing the water gun if Lonnie ever happened to be in Philadelphia.

"But don't make a special trip," the guy said.

Lonnie made a special trip.

In his wife's suitcase, he carried a new prototype. He unpacked it, filled the tank with water, pumped the gun until the air pressure was good and high, and . . .

HOOSH!

Kids everywhere agreed with that "Wow!" Lonnie's water gun, called the Super Soaker, became a smash hit. In no time there were Super Soakers in backyards and on beaches, in parks and on playgrounds. Each sale of a Super Soaker put a little money into Lonnie's pocket.

All those hours—all those years—that Lonnie spent in his workshop had paid off big-time. Now he could afford to do just about anything he wanted.

So what did Lonnie do?

He got a bigger workshop, which is where you'll find him today. Because facing challenges, solving problems, and building things are what Lonnie Johnson loves to do. And his ideas just keep on flowing.

AUTHOR'S NOTE

A SUPER SOAKER uses a pump to compress the air found in its water reservoir, which puts pressure on the water. When the trigger is pulled, the pressurized water can escape and . . . WHOOSH! If you search the internet for "how Super Soakers work," you'll find a lot more about what goes on inside Lonnie Johnson's most famous invention.* But if you want to better understand how Lonnie Johnson himself works, then you'll put this book down, step away from the computer screen, and get permission to take something apart so you can see those kinds of goings-on for yourself. You might even start with a Super Soaker.

This book began with a lunchtime conversation I had with a couple of librarians in Texas. They had recently gone to a seminar where attendees were asked to draw a picture of a scientist. The most common image was of a guy who resembled Albert Einstein—lab coat, wild hair, white skin. The point of the exercise was to draw attention to the fact that scientists are more diverse than that.

The lesson those librarians learned rubbed off on me, and by dinnertime I had found the story of the African American rocket scientist who invented the Super Soaker.

What was most appealing to me about Lonnie Johnson's story was the fact that it was still unfolding. He didn't just take his Super Soaker money and retire young. Instead, he directed it toward hands-on efforts to solve one of the most important engineering puzzles of our day. His mission? To efficiently harness heat energy—from the sun and other sources—in order to generate the electricity we need without polluting the planet.

I loved talking with Lonnie Johnson for this book. I have never laughed as hard during an interview as I did when we discussed his work on Linex and how his family "put up with" his efforts—or rather, how they encouraged him. It's no surprise that today, even as he continues his own work, Lonnie Johnson makes time to encourage the efforts of tomorrow's scientists and engineers.

I hope that this book will encourage them, too.

---

* Throughout his life Lonnie Johnson has sometimes worked alone and at other times as part of a team. The water gun that began in his bathroom got some help along the way from a builder of prototypes named Bruce D'Andrade. The names of both men appear on the original patent for what became known as the Super Soaker. However, Bruce's widow, Mary Ann, told me that her husband considered Lonnie to be the inventor.

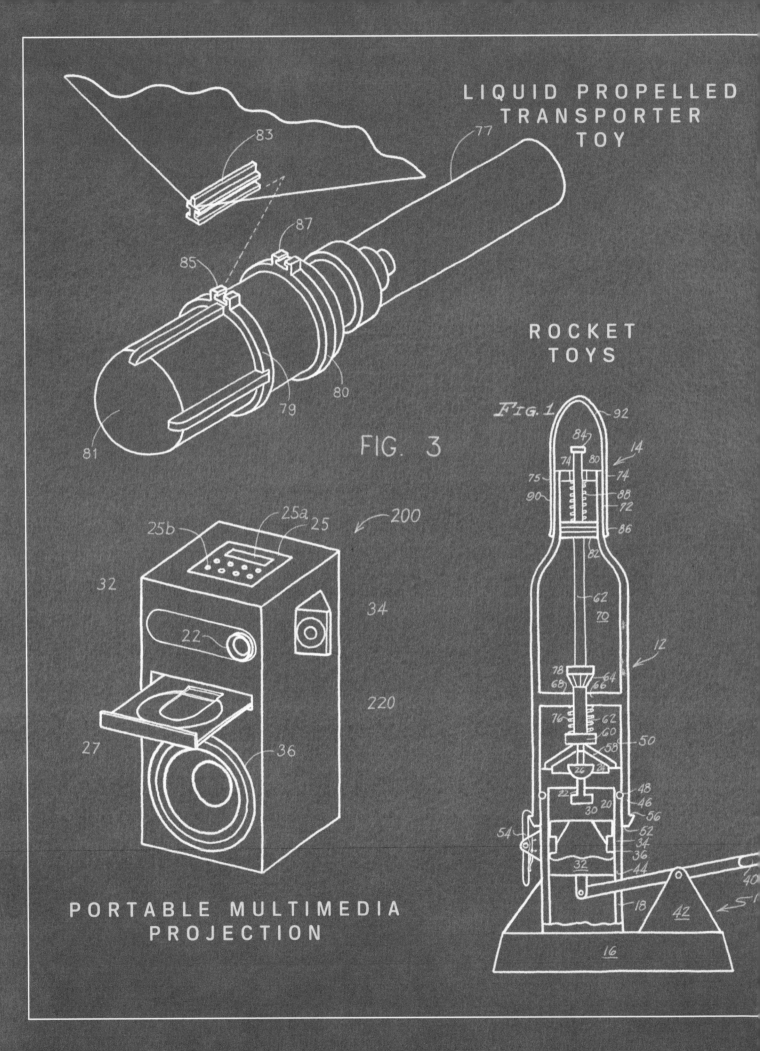

LIQUID PROPELLED
TRANSPORTER
TOY

ROCKET
TOYS

FIG. 3

PORTABLE MULTIMEDIA
PROJECTION